A Suzuki Parent's Diary

Or
How I Survived My First 10,000 Twinkles

A Suzuki Parent's Diary

Or
How I Survived
My First 10,000
Twinkles

by Carroll Morris

 A Senzay® Edition

by Ability Development Associates, Inc.
subsidiary of Accura Music, Inc.
Athens, Ohio, U.S.A.

ISBN: 0-918194-14-8
Cover Design: Paul Bradford
Drawings: Jane Jellings
Typesetting: Quick Printer, Athens, Ohio
Lithographed in the United States of America by
Lawhead Press, Inc., Athens, Ohio

Table of Contents

Editor's Comment

Teachers and parents who are involved in Suzuki violin programs may notice that certain teaching procedures recounted in this book are different than those that they use. Such variations, frequently regional, need not be cause for concern. Suzuki pedagogy continues to evolve as teachers find more effective ways of presenting material and motivating young children. Teachers are urged to continue to upgrade their teaching skills by attending workshops and institutes. Through observation and discussion, new technics are evaluated and frequently adopted. Less effective—even inefficient—procedures can be dropped or modified. Because each child is different, every teacher must be flexible, creative and constantly growing.

Foreword

What is it like to be a Suzuki parent? Are some people just "naturals," whereas others have a lot of difficulty? Do some have problems that are overwhelming, yet others follow the philosophy of *Nurtured By Love* and *Ability Development From Age Zero* and find the Suzuki method to be a joyful experience?

Most parents of Suzuki students discover that they go through stages. For awhile they harbor their doubts and frustrations in secret, fearing that they are the only ones that are not able to make the system work as well as they believe it should. Then, through meeting with other parents, they learn to their amazement and relief that 1) there are rough spots in the road for everyone, and 2) the problems are solvable, and with their solution the real joy of being a Suzuki parent follows.

Carroll Morris, with her humorous style, recounts the consternation, the work, and the thrill of that first year as a very unseasoned Suzuki parent. Through anecdotes, she reveals her innermost thoughts and feelings in a delightful light-hearted style.

For parents considering the Suzuki approach for their children, this book will chart a course of expectations. No lecture or text book could convey more effectively to parents a sense of what being "in Suzuki" involves.

For an experienced parent, the book will serve as a reminder of those poignant events in their life that were similar. Laughter comes more easily now.

For all, the book is a well disguised précis of child rearing and child psychology as incorporated in those first years of the Suzuki "experience."

The Suzuki method, as with life itself, is not a thing or a status — it is a journey. I hope that the reader finds Mrs. Morris' account of that first year's journey as pleasurable as I did.

Lorraine Fink

October, 1984

Preface

A few months ago, a woman called me for information about Suzuki violin. Poor lady. The information she wanted could have been given in three minutes, but I turned on my "Suzuki is marvelous" tape, and let her have it — beginning to end.

Well, that night I had a horrible dream. An imposing figure dressed in white and carrying a transparent violin approached me. Waving his crystal bow at me, he asked menacingly, "Do you remember what you said just one year ago today about 'Suzuki mothers'?"

Quickly I did a re-run trying to get back to last year. When I realized what he was referring to, I nodded reluctantly.

"Well, what did you say?"

"I said that all Suzuki mothers sound like a recording of 'The Wonderful World of Suzuki.' "

"And how did you sound today?" The eyes were penetrating. There was no escape.

I lowered my eyes and mumbled, "Exactly the same."

The figure waved the golden-haired bow and from nowhere a ream of paper appeared. "In penance, you shall now write the truth about your first year's experience as a Suzuki mother. The *whole* truth!"

"The *whole* truth?" I asked doubtfully.

He didn't answer, but he really didn't need to. I got the message. And though like all midnight mirages he was gone with the morning light, I couldn't forget his injunction.

So I did it, and here it is, in black and white and blood-red. May it help when the E string breaks, the sponge and rubber bands disappear, your child develops sudden-onset arthritis of the fingers and you wonder, "Why am I doing this, anyway?"

"Suzuki?"

The Invitation

September 4

Today Carrie brought home a slip from school about Suzuki violin. I confess to some degree of confusion. I thought Suzuki made motorcycles, not music.

P.S.   Now I've got it . . . it just took me a while to remember. Suzuki is the guy with the little violinists. I saw his picture once in *Time* magazine. Seems to me his students don't learn to read notes. Sounds suspiciously like the "Think" method used by Professor Harold Hill in *Music Man*!

September 5

In spite of the image I have of Professor Hill leading a bunch of little fiddlers in "Seventy-six Trombones," I was intrigued by the idea of Suzuki violin all last night. So I wrote a note to the music teacher asking for whatever information she could give me, and sent it with Carrie this morning.

September 8

Boy, was Mrs. Wirth ready for me! Carrie brought home a lot of handouts today—in fact, a whole packet of information. There's a lengthy handout entitled "Questions and Answers Regarding Suzuki Instruction in Upland Schools"; excerpts from something called "A Brief Summary of Talent Education," by Sanford Reuning; a registration sheet and a sheet with the title "So You Want to be a Suzuki Parent."

I made the mistake of reading the one about parents first. I had the vague notion I'd sign Carrie up, sit back and watch her be wonderful! Hah! According to this, *I* have to be wonderful—patient, enthusiastic, involved, etc., etc., etc.

Actually, that last adjective puts it in a nutshell—involved. I'm supposed to go to every lesson, individual and group, and help Carrie with every practice during the week. Sounds to me like I might as well be taking the lessons myself.

Oh, one other thing. The kids *do* learn to read notes, thank heavens. But only after they are fairly proficient. I guess in the case of a very young child, it might be a very long time before he starts note-reading, but eventually he will.

Still, the idea sits a little uncomfortably with me. After all, I had a piano teacher who would roll over if she heard anyone say it was all right to hear new music before playing it. She *never* wanted us to hear what a song was like. That would make it "too easy," as she said.

So, I guess what's called for here is a "willing suspension of disbelief," at least long enough to give the program a try.

Carrie told me her friend Amanda plays "Suzuki," so I asked her mother to tell me a little about it. I wonder if all parents get evangelistic when their children take up Suzuki violin. Amanda's mom couldn't stop talking about how she loved it and how Amanda loved it and what it had done for their relationship.

I guess that is what really caught my interest, the way she kept saying that Suzuki violin had made a difference in the way the two of them felt about each other. I have been wishing that Carrie and I had something we could do together. Maybe this is it.

Oh, she did suggest that I read *Nurtured by Love*, a book by Dr. Suzuki. She declined lending me her copy. It was autographed.

P.S.   I've been thinking about what taking piano lessons did for me and my mom — not exactly what Dr. Suzuki had in mind, I don't think. And what's to guarantee anything better for Carrie and me?

September 11

I've been talking to a lot of ladies whose children are "into Suzuki." Some of these ladies I have known casually for years, and I never knew their children were playing violin. Seems like Suzuki people are popping up everywhere. Why is it I never noticed before?

And they *are* evangelistic — no doubt about it. They all say the same thing about the program: that it is the best thing that has come into their lives and that they just love it.

They have the Suzuki teacher on a pedestal, too. And no wonder. She's "patient, kind, tolerant, supportive, inspired and the reason they just love going to the lessons."

How can a person resist such propaganda?

They have the Suzuki teacher on a pedestal.

September 12

I know someone who can resist the propaganda —
Fred! I told him all the interesting and exciting things I
had heard about Suzuki violin and he said, "Sounds
good, but what's the other side of the picture?" Well, that
stumped me but good, because I don't know any other
side.

Honestly, no one I have talked to so far has mentioned
any problems. But there must be something on the other
side of the ledger. There always is.

I guess I will find out soon enough, because in spite of
skepticism, Fred is all for getting Carrie started. He is a
bit concerned about whether it will be too much for her to
handle at a time when she'll also be adjusting to first
grade. But we have decided to give it a try.

The Commitment

September 13

I sent in Carrie's registration today. It sounds like such a wonderful program. And from what I've been told, having this instruction available through the public school system is quite unusual. Still, I felt like I was signing away my life when I put my name on the dotted line. Just look at this!

I understand when I sign this registration I agree to:

1. *obtain a proper-sized instrument for the child.*
2. *purchase the appropriate music instruction books and records.*
3. *encourage my child to practice daily and complete required assignments.*
4. *see that my child attends required practices and concerts.*
5. *familiarize myself with the talent education philosophy by reading such books as Shinichi Suzuki's* Nurtured By Love.
6. *attend the parent meetings and discussions.*
7. *be in attendance at all lesson sessions for my child.*

Sounds like a big order, and I have to deal with item one when Carrie gets home tonight. She wanted to rush out and get her violin at 8 o'clock this morning, but I convinced her that we had to wait at least until after school. She'll be home in 30 minutes. *What do I know about buying violins?*

September 14

Much to Carrie's disappointment, we didn't buy a violin yesterday. I didn't feel that I know enough about it yet, and I couldn't remember everything Mrs. Wirth had told me. So I visited with Amanda's mother last night. Marie — that's her name — gave me some really good ideas.

From what she told me, I have two options. One is to rent a violin from a local store for a trial period of three months. After that time, the violin can either be returned or purchased.

I can see a couple of advantages to buying from a music store. One is that I wouldn't need to have the total purchase price on hand. And with the cost of instruments going up like everything else, that could be important. The other is the trade-in program Marie told me about. Most companies will accept a violin back and allow a percentage of the purchase price to be applied toward a new violin.

"Then when Carrie outgrows hers, you can trade it in," said Marie.

Outgrows it? Oh, help. Shoes and coats are bad enough, but *violins?*

Anyway, the other option is to buy a violin from the list of those offered for sale by other Suzuki parents. (You guessed it, outgrown ones!) Mrs. Wirth says it is possible to get a good violin for less by buying from the list. And of course, one also avoids the interest on time payments. (That's Fred's contribution.)

September 18

Well, we're the proud owners of a one-tenth size violin.

We checked the list of violins for sale to see who was selling a one-tenth—the size suggested by Mrs. Wirth—and we ended up buying one from the Eglers, who had just bought a one-fourth size for their little boy.

It was a delightful experience. We got what seems to be a nice violin at a price we could afford, and got acquainted with someone else in the program. The Eglers had Andy play for us, which really delighted Carrie. I was impressed by the fact that he seemed to think it was *fun* to perform.

Anyhow, Carrie was thrilled when they let her "try on" the one-tenth. She mimicked Andy's posture and they checked to see if she could curl her fingers around the scroll without straightening out her arm. She could, and the Eglers assured us that it was the right size for her.

I hope so. As far as I could tell it didn't look too big. And they said that it had good tone for a student violin. Well, that may be true with Andy playing, but when Carrie drew the bow across the strings, all I could think about was alley cats.

Lessons Begin

We had our first group lesson today, and it was really something! The music room was filled with all the beginners, moms, and assorted brothers and sisters. The beginners, ages 5-7, stood in front of the blackboard while the moms and siblings sat in a semicircle facing them.

We were all excited and anxious to get going, ready to learn great things. And the first thing Mrs. Wirth taught us was *how to bow*! Truly! They bowed for us and we clapped for them! "Feet together, arms to the side, bend and say 'hippopotamus.'" I assume the 'hippopotamus' will disappear when they get used to holding their bows long enough to dispel the image of bobbing for apples.

We learned some other things as well: the position for the hand when holding the bow, some bow exercises and how to position the feet for rest position and playing position. But the main thing I learned is that when Dr. Suzuki said to teach in small steps, he really meant SMALL!

September 21

Carrie really loves the bow games—making the window shade go up and down, and the rocket take off. And "Bow Bunny" is a favorite: making a circle with the two middle fingers and thumb while extending the two outer fingers makes a "bunny." She picks up pencils, *Legos*, etc. with her "bunny."

I also have her go up and down the stairs and around the kitchen table with her "violin" in a good "sandwich", chin and shoulder being the bread, the "violin" the filling. Actually, the violin in this case is a book. I'm not crazy enough to let her do that with the real article yet.

A bow-hand "bunny"

15

September 23

I've done some checking, and it seems that it really is quite unusual for a school district to offer training in Suzuki violin as part of the music program (actually, it isn't just violin; viola and cello are taught as well). More often, Suzuki teachers are affiliated with a university or a music school or have their own studio. So it is a special opportunity to live in this school district.

Kids can sign up for the program from kindergarten to grade three. The program goes through sixth grade, but after third grade, beginning string students usually start a note-reading program and go into orchestra.

The lines aren't that clear, though. The Suzuki kids also start note-reading in third grade and play in orchestra as well. And since both Mrs. Wirth and Miss Strang, the orchestra teacher, have training in Suzuki violin, they are doing a lot of innovative things to make the Suzuki repertoire part of the general string program. From what I hear, this approach has resulted in some excellent string concerts on the elementary level.

September 24

Carrie had her first individual lesson today. Mrs. Wirth showed her how to stand in rest position and in playing position, and reviewed the bow-hold she had learned in group.

Carrie actually played "Mississippi River" on the A string and then on the E string! Mrs. Wirth gave us a fingering sheet and we are supposed to sing the fingering several times a day and practice the first phrase — A A E E 1 1 E. But only after practicing changing the bow from A to E several days.

You should have seen Carrie's left hand! She will never wash it again, so she says. Mrs. Wirth drew two little eyes on the tip of Carrie's thumb to help remind her that the thumb should be straight up. "Keep the eyes looking at the ceiling," she said. Then she drew a little face on the nail of Carrie's first finger. That way, when Carrie puts it down on the E string, the little face is looking at her. She thinks it's wonderful!

September 25

We're singing the fingering sheet for "Twinkle" several times a day, A A E E 1 1 E, etc. I can see how that will make a difference when Carrie starts to play the song. She will have the fingering already in her head and will not have to be so consciously involved with that aspect when she picks up her violin.

But at this point our practices consist mostly of "games," like the "rest position-playing position" game, which basically is getting the feet together in rest position, and both the left foot and nose pointing north (or east or west, as the case may be) in playing position.

What amazes me is how much Carrie needs to learn before she starts to play. And how much fun it can be to learn it.

September 27

We're getting ourselves organized around here. Our weekly schedule includes a 10-minute individual lesson (one real disadvantage of the training through the school is the limited time per student), a group lesson each week and a district-wide play-in once a month.

So far, Carrie has not been to a district play-in and won't for a while. As soon as she can play all the "Twinkles" well and perhaps "Lightly Row," we'll start going.

I'm sure glad for the piano lessons I took as a child. I don't feel completely lost, but violins are a real mystery to me. I would be more confident if I knew some basic terminology, and more about the care and feeding of the thing. Perhaps the parents' meeting I'm going to tomorrow night will fill in the gaps.

September 28

Well, I know what a fingerboard is, what a tailpiece is and how to tune a violin, thanks to the parents' meeting last night. I must say it was comforting to be in a room full of people as insecure about violins as I. We don't get much of a chance to talk to each other at our children's group lessons—we just commiserate silently. But all of that non-verbal communication became very, very verbal last night. We talked and talked and talked. It was great.

It was also nice to have some seasoned "Suzuki mothers" there as well. They were very encouraging. Most had gone through much the same things we were experiencing.

One of them made an interesting comment. She said that according to Dr. Suzuki, every child can learn to "hear" A. If he sings what he thinks is A every day and then corrects the pitch, he will eventually have that pitch "in his ear." Sounds possible, but right now, I'm content to blow my pitch pipe!

September 30

I guess you could call this the "honeymoon." We're all excited, playing the tape diligently, practicing a couple of times a day. Having the violin in the house is almost like having a new baby. We've tuned it, wiped it down, carried it, done everything but burp it!

And was it ever hard to keep my cool the first time Carrie dropped it! Thank goodness this violin is a used one. It is already somewhat chipped and scratched, and that seems to help me be a little less paranoid about the bumps it takes. I guess it's like having a new car. The first scratch attracts a lot of attention, but subsequent scratches are hardly even noticed.

October 3

Another week, another group lesson. I know the names of most of the kids in our group and their mothers too. There are two boys and four girls, all in kindergarten or first grade. What a motley crew—violins pointing in all directions, feet everywhere, and concentration nowhere. But Mrs. Wirth helps each one of them individually as well as having group activities. At least during that time, they are paying attention. And who knows? They may be getting more out of the rest of it than I think.

I do have to chuckle when I see mothers grimace as their child makes a mistake or acts a bit silly. I'm sure I do the same.

October 7

I've been reading *Nurtured by Love* and it is almost embarrassing to admit, but I'm converted.

It is gratifying to read the philosophy of a man who believes so whole-heartedly in the intrinsic worth of children; who believes that good, beautiful and loving qualities are within every child, waiting to be brought out.

I read the book thinking of Carrie, but then I realized that I would like someone to give me that same affirmation. Can I give to Carrie what I need myself?

At our first group lesson

October 10

I went to group lesson today with one question on my mind. Would Suzanne play or not? Suzanne is a beautiful first grader, blond and blue-eyed in the way of Scandinavian Minnesotans, and painfully shy. At our first group lesson, she spent the whole time clinging to her mother, those blue eyes huge and bright with tears. And the second lesson was no different. So I watched them come in today, wondering how Suzanne's mother would handle things. Slowly and with some resistance on Suzanne's part, they came into the room. Suzanne's mother was gentle, but firm, and together they came over to the semicircle of chairs where the mothers were sitting.

The mother — I think her name is Caroline — got out the violin and had Suzanne tighten and rosin the bow, which she did willingly. Then she told Suzanne it was time to join the other children at the front of the room.

A flash of fear crossed the child's face and she grabbed her mother's dress and shook her head in opposition. I believe she was genuinely disturbed, not just playing a game for the sake of attention. Though my first response would have been to say, "Now look here, we spent $XXXX on this violin and you jolly well better play!" Caroline didn't pressure Suzanne. She encouraged her, but didn't force her. Suzanne spent another group lesson sitting on her mother's lap.

October 11

Whoever thinks "Twinkle, Twinkle Little Star" is a simple folk tune is nuts. Boy, is there a lot Carrie has to know before she can play that song and all the variations well. Fortunately, she doesn't realize that what she is doing is complicated! I really use the "Stop-Prepare" idea a lot. Carrie stops before a problem spot and prepares before going on. That way she doesn't play it wrong. (Pardon me. That is not quite the way it works. I should have said that she stops and prepares when I am right there with her to remind her. Her own goal is to play the darn thing through once. Who cares whether it's right or wrong!)

Mrs. Wirth says the old notion of practice makes perfect isn't the whole story. "Practicing a section wrong just results in a perfectly wrong section. Only slow, careful, stop-prepare practice will eventually produce the desired results."

October 13

Carrie wouldn't play today. Her neck hurt. I suppose it is quite uncomfortable to crane one's neck around like that and then squeeze a hard object between chin and shoulder. We do have a sponge for her, but it doesn't seem to alleviate all the discomfort.

Well, she just complained and complained. No matter what I said or did to get the lesson going in a positive way, it just didn't work. So, I just said, "I see that you can't play today, so let's put the violin away, and instead, we'll spend the time listening to the tape together."

It worked for today, but what will happen tomorrow? There really is no magic in the Professor Hill method, no magic in listening without practicing.

P.S.   It was back to practice as usual the next day. Thankfully, a crisis had been avoided.

October 14

It's interesting to see how Fred is handling all of this. He tends to be somewhat detached, but he is aware of what's going on and likes what I have told him about the philosophy. And he is always glad to have Carrie play for him. I haven't talked him into going to a lesson yet, but perhaps that is unfair. He knows nothing about music, and although that's not a prerequisite, he says he would be uncomfortable, and would rather not.

That's O.K. He supports us in other ways, and as long as I am the one who helps Carrie practice, I'm happy to go to the lessons.

October 17

Suzanne played today! I can't believe it! Joining the group with about the same confidence a fawn would join a circle of wolves, she set her violin and bow down and did the games along with the others. She even stood and played "Mississippi River."

Oh, my heart goes out to her! All the time she was playing her eyes were communicating her distress, but she played anyway! I just wonder who worked the miracle. Suzanne herself, or her mother, or Mrs. Wirth? Or all of them together?

I understand in a new way Dr. Suzuki's statement about giving each child the time she needs. My approach would have turned the lesson into a battleground and then nobody would have had a chance to "win." But Caroline's patience and understanding, *and* gentle firmness turned the corner. Hurrah for Caroline, and hurrah for Suzanne.

October 21

I'd like to know who called Variation 2 "Popcorn and Candy." It is anything but sweet, in fact it has been a real pain. We used the old "divide and conquer" principle. Practicing the bowing, first — singing it, bowing over her shoulder, bowing while I did the fingerings — anything to isolate the bowing. Then, we played for a long time just on the A and E strings. But we finally got it!

A suggestion from Mrs. Wirth helped: she said to sing outrageous combinations throughout the variation, such as "peanuts and donuts," or "milk shakes and pizza."

Variation Two

October 28

We have clapped and tapped and sung the rhythms till we're blue — "Mississippi River," "Popcorn and Candy," "Grasshopper," and "Mississippi, Mississippi"! Sometimes I hold the violin while she bows, then I bow while she practices the fingering. Other times she practices the rhythms over her shoulder with the bow (hair side up) and sometimes we even shake hands to the rhythms.

Oh, another thing we've done that's fun is to see who can find other words with the same rhythm, like we did for "Popcorn and Candy"; "Grandmother, Grandfather," for "Grasshopper," or "Minneapolis, Minnesota," for "Mississippi, Mississippi." That makes it personal, and Carrie didn't mind the repetition so much when we added a new twist.

All of this is leading up to an announcement: We are starting to sing the fingerings for — are you ready? — "LIGHTLY ROW"!!! Carrie is so excited! And so am I.

That doesn't mean that we can forget the "Twinkles," though. I guess Carrie will be playing them forever. But then, I remind myself that one of the things I like about the program is that the repertoire is meant to be played over and over again. It makes so much sense to learn fewer songs and improve them by review than to learn something new each week, something that will never be played again.

So, welcome to the family, "Mississippi River."

Parents, Practice, Patience, and More

October 29

I know that competition between kids (PARENTS?) is not part of the Suzuki approach, but I find myself falling into the "And what piece is so-and-so on" trap at times. It is pretty hard not to get into that, especially at group lessons when my child seems to be the only one with her scroll pointing at the toe of her sneaker. (I wonder if that's because she's the only one I'm looking at?)

And it's not just the kids at group lesson that are drawn into comparison with Carrie. It's also the cute, round-faced Oriental child *playing a concerto at age 6.* And that child is no myth either. She's a hundred little violinists who never scratch when they are supposed to be playing, who don't step on their rosin and smash it into the rug, who never lose their sponge, and who always listen to the teacher instead of watching the garbage man empty the dumpster outside the music room window.

November 1

I can see now why everyone is so enthusiastic about Mrs. Wirth. She is unfailingly kind, encouraging and loving. She praises what Carrie has done, then asks her to do better. I'm not sure how she does it, but she asks Carrie to improve without disparaging what she *has* accomplished.

And then she says things like, "Isn't it nice that you have a mother who can help you so well?"

Sounds like a set piece, but it isn't. She truly means what she says, and knowing that helps me feel more confident and encouraged, ready to go another week.

November 4

I recently talked to a Suzuki mom who is taking her preschoolers to a private Suzuki instructor. She told me a little about how the lessons go and what they do at home. She said it often takes a *year* for a preschooler to learn the positions, the bow hold and the "Twinkles"!

I am truly humbled. If I thought Carrie and I were taking small steps, I wasn't entirely right. There are degrees of small, I've discovered.

November 7

I thought I was going into cardiac arrest in group lesson today. For some reason the kids were antsy and they kept leaving the group and coming to where the mothers were sitting. Which meant they had to thread their way through all the violins lying on the floor. Only they didn't seem to be paying the slightest bit of attention to the position of their feet relative to the violins! They jumped or stepped over them seemingly completely oblivious, while I was in the throes of an anxiety attack!

The patron saint of Suzuki violinists must have been watching over us, because all the violins were intact at the end of the lesson!

November 9

The patron saint doesn't always protect violins, I've discovered. Someone told me a story about a friend who rented a very expensive quarter-size violin because of its unusually beautiful tone. And she has been extra concerned about the safety of this valuable instrument.

Well, at one of her daughter's group lessons, the kids all had their violins on the floor and were doing something that included jumping. She said, "You know, I really don't want to have Anne's violin on the floor while the kids are doing that."

"Oh, don't worry. We do this all the time and we've never had any accidents," was the reply. (File under "Famous Last Words.")

The friend went out of the room for a few minutes and when she returned, she noticed that everyone was looking rather strange. Then she saw the violin, which was also looking rather strange! It was in two pieces. Anne had landed on it and the fingerboard had broken completely off.

Why is it that well-meaning persons always have a horror story tailored to fit the current anxiety?

P.S. The violin was repaired and sounds fine!

November 10

I've had a real blow. I read that Dr. Suzuki doesn't like the word "patience" because it implies "controlled frustration." Here I've been feeling virtuous because I was managing to be patient!

Sigh.

I guess the ideal is to be truly loving.

Patience

November 12

I've been fiddling around with Carrie's violin lately. (Oops! You'll have to excuse that. I'm not normally so punny.) What a strange feeling trying to play that little thing! I wanted to experience some of what Carrie is experiencing when she is learning a new song, but for that, I really needed to try a full-size violin. So, I borrowed one from another trusting mother.

Well, I jumped right in, of course. What else would a compulsive person do? I put that violin in a "sandwich" so tight it was like a vise. I got a perfect grip on the bow, and I played, more or less, for a half hour.

Let me tell you, I will never be the same again! My neck is so stiff I feel like a figure on an Egyptian vase, captured forever in playing position. I've never really understood what I was asking Carrie to do before. It is not an easy task and I am really impressed with what she has done. Getting in good position, holding the bow correctly, and then playing a song is quite a feat. Bless her, she's doing great. I, on the other hand, may not live the night.

Captured forever in playing position

November 13

Carrie and I are still trying to figure out a good time for practicing and listening. I want her to help make the choice, so she can feel like she's part of the decision. The listening can probably be a bit more spontaneous than the practicing, especially since we have the tape and Carrie can take the tape recorder with her wherever she goes. So far, meal time or bedtime seems to be the preferred time for listening.

But the practice time needs to be set, I think. That way it can become a habit. For us, right before Carrie leaves for school seems to be best, since we just don't get it done if we wait until after school.

Also, someone suggested that setting a definite limit to the practice time is a good idea. I agree. When Carrie is doing well, I have the tendency to say, "Oh, that was great! Let's do it one more time," until she's fed up and tired and a good lesson has been turned into a drag. Works the other way, too. When she has a problem, I tend to work it to death. I think if I let Carrie know before we start that her lesson will be done after x number of repetitions of a, b, and c she will be more willing, and I will be too.

November 14

Today was our first day at the regular group lesson. No more beginner's group for us, even though all Carrie can play really well are the "Twinkles." She is making progress, though. She can play all of "Lightly Row" — *slowly*.

But let me tell you, she was totally unprepared for the tempo these kids play at. She was behind on the "Twinkles" all the way through and "Lightly Row" was a disaster. She kept jumping and skipping to try to stay up.

She didn't seem to be discouraged at being behind, though. She was fascinated with the older kids and the songs they were playing. She has her favorites from the tape and whenever Mrs. Wirth had the group play one of them, Carrie would look at me and smile.

November 20

Is there really a difference between what can be asked of American children and what can be asked of children growing up in Japan? Is our culture so different? Is our life-style so different? There must be some factors that have to be taken into account. Dr. Suzuki himself seems to recognize some difference. He says that everyone ought to practice four hours a day, "But Americans get a 50 percent discount!"

P.S.   What would he think of the additional discount we take?

There's Going to be a Concert!

November 21

There's going to be a concert! Carrie's excited even though she'll just be playing "Twinkle Tune" and "Lightly Row." We went to a play-through tonight and the concert will be Tuesday night.

You can guess what a play-through is — playing through the numbers to be performed at the concert. But there's more to it than that. The kids have to be grouped together according to their most difficult concert piece, and shown the rows they are to stand in. Mrs. Wirth has marked the rows with masking tape and has individual name cards for each child. Can you imagine the work?

Once the kids had their violins tuned — quite a process in itself — and were in their places, the play-through got underway.

Carrie says that playing in a group is a lot different from playing alone. She can't hear herself as well when others are playing. She also says the songs sound different when accompanied. She had some difficulty with concert etiquette, too — watching the teacher, listening for the introduction, bowing on cue, etc.

But the biggest difficulty she has is keeping up with the tempo. The songs are played a lot faster than we have been practicing them up to now. I mentioned this to another mother and she suggested I buy an accompaniment tape. She has one, and her little boy plays along with it a lot. As a result, he has no trouble with the tempo. Mrs. Wirth is amazing. She seems to have an unending reserve of patience. I'm wondering if there isn't an "ORDER OF SUZUKI SAINTS" she could be inducted into.

P.S.   Mustn't forget to get a blue skirt and white blouse for Carrie. Standard performing dress for our group, I understand.

November 22

What an evening. I laughed, cried, cringed and felt proud, both singly and simultaneously.

Even the preliminaries were interesting. All the kids lined up for tuning, though how anyone could hear a note is beyond me, since those already tuned were playing everything from "Lully Gavotte" (one of the concert numbers) to "Twinkle" to "Boil Them Cabbage Down," a fiddling tune Mrs. Wirth teaches the kids for fun.

After tuning, the kids started to find their positions from name cards taped to the floor, and some actually *sat down* where they were supposed to be. But then the "see how close you can come to stepping on the violins without actually mashing them" routine began, as kids left their places to get drinks or tell their parents some *important thing.*

The concert started right on time, a minor miracle in itself. But then came the real miracle. Such good music from such young people. I especially enjoyed hearing the Bach *"Double."* (Mrs. Wirth tickles the kids' funny bones by calling it the "Dach Bubble"!) Even the songs I've heard a thousand times were fun to listen to. Repetition doesn't lessen the appeal of good music.

But while the more advanced repertoire was being played, the younger kids were really putting on a show. "Three-ring" doesn't begin to describe that circus!

There were the inevitable nose pickers and hair suckers, whisperers and gigglers. Then there were the more inventive types. Like the little girl who took her name card, tore it into small pieces, and put them underneath her skirt (she was sitting on the floor). Then she proceeded to take them out one at a time and bestow them upon the favored few who were sitting around her!

Nevertheless, when the younger children got up to

play, it was very special. I never thought hearing the "Twinkles" would make me cry!

After the concert, we went to an ice cream parlor — not a very unique idea, I found. There were at least 15 blue and white kids there, all eating ice cream.

P.S.   When Carrie stood up to play, her sweater pulled up and her belly-button was on display the whole time. Either get a bigger sweater or make a jumper.

Get a longer sweater or make a jumper.

December 5

Well, it happened. The world didn't fall apart, the bill was only $13.00 and I found out that violins are fairly sturdy.

A few days ago, Carrie got mad at Matt, her little brother, and she bonked him on the head with her violin. It didn't seem to rattle his brains any, but the violin sure got rattled!

I'm not kidding! After we got everything settled down, Carrie picked up her violin to put it away, and it actually did rattle. Something was loose inside, and whenever she moved the violin from right to left, it would roll from side to side. We couldn't figure out what had happened.

Shows what I know about violins. I had no idea there was such a thing as a sound post under the bridge. I also had no idea how potentially damaging it can be when one is not in position. Not knowing what was going on, we had not loosened the strings, which Mrs. Wirth says is the first thing to do in such a case. When tightened, the strings put tremendous pressure on the bridge, and the sound post helps support this pressure.

Mrs. Wirth gave us the name of a reputable repairman and he had it fixed within a week.

P.S.   Yes, I did have a talk with Carrie and Matt. Henceforth, they will pick some other object for head-bonking.

December 6

Fred has started practicing the "Twinkles" now and then. Carrie loves to see her dad play. She can tell him exactly how to stand, how to hold the bow, how to make a violin sandwich: "Hug yourself with your left hand. Now, put the violin on your shoulder. No, not that way, this way. Now put your chin on the chin rest and squeeze. Oh, Daddy! You're letting it slip! It's supposed to be level!"

They have a lot of fun together, and Carrie's playing and position is never as good as when she shows her dad how to do it right.

December 7

Our group is smaller by one.

One of the little boys, Scott, no longer comes. I had been aware that his mother was very tense during group practice, anxious for him to do everything right, frustrated when he didn't. And she would even call to him from her seat, "Scott, point your toe." Or, "Scott, bend your thumb."

Not that I can sit there totally disinterested while Carrie does weird things, but I have not pointed out her defects so that all could hear. (Yes, I do admit to a bit of pantomime when I can catch her attention, but I hope it is in a positive, encouraging way.)

I guess I feel a bit ambivalent about the fact that they quit. On the one hand, their experience in Suzuki did not seem to be positive; it seemed, in fact, to be a point of conflict. Quitting removed that source of conflict.

On the other hand, if what happened in group is indicative of their total relationship, then they need to have the influence of something positive in it. Perhaps by sticking with Suzuki, they could have learned how to interact differently.

That's one thing I like about the program. It is based on a positive, loving way of relating to the world and to people. I'm no saint, and Carrie is no prodigy, but the ideal behind the program is helping us do something really wonderful together.

December 14

We've had a lot of opportunities to play this month. Mrs. Wirth arranged for the students to play at some nursing homes, and Carrie wanted to go, so we did. It's amazing how the elderly people responded to the children, and vice versa. I guess it was because the children could sense how much they were appreciated and loved.

We also played at a big shopping center. It was exciting, but not nearly so personal.

Many of the beginners had taken some extra time to learn "Jolly Old Saint Nicholas" from a fingering sheet — Carrie included. She learned it so quickly! And I think it is a lot harder than "Lightly Row." Of course, it isn't up to tempo, but Mrs. Wirth takes it a little slowly for their sake. Nobody seems to mind.

So, on Christmas Eve we'll start a new tradition — Carrie on the violin. She'll play "Jolly Old Saint Nicholas" and "Twinkle, Twinkle Little Star." That's appropriate, isn't it? After all, there was a star that special night.

We've Hit the January Doldrums

January 6

We've hit the January doldrums. I guess I knew they would come sooner or later, but I was not prepared for them when they came.

Christmas vacation did it. We just let all our scheduling go, relaxed, slept in, did something fun every day and didn't practice or even listen to the tape very often. BIG MISTAKE. We should have listened at least.

Now getting back on schedule is really tough. Seems as though we almost have to learn some songs over again. What a waste of effort. And as silly as it seems, even turning on the tape is a big deal. How are we ever going to get back to where we were?

January 9

This is terrible. When we were practicing and listening and really into the program, I could see progress and I was optimistic and enthusiastic. Now I feel as if progress is an illusion. All I can see are the problems. All I can hear are the sour notes.

I feel frustrated that Carrie is not a prodigy and then I feel rotten because I am not a good Suzuki mother. What a guilt trip! If I don't find a way out of this, I'm going to quit.

January 10

Boy, was I in the dumps yesterday! But, things aren't so bad today. Mrs. Wirth gave us the go-ahead on a new song, "Song of the Wind." Bless her heart. We needed a fresh start and this gives us the opportunity to get off on the right foot again. And Carrie was more than ready for it in any case.

January 14

I read *Nurtured by Love* again this week, and I found myself feeling better as I read. I need to read this often. It reminds me of my reasons for starting Suzuki violin in the first place.

But you know, I also need to provide for myself all the things I have been trying to provide for Carrie. I need to give *myself* praise for the things I do. I need to give *myself* the time I need to succeed. I need to remember that there is always tomorrow.

January 20

You would not believe what I just found out! Fred hates to listen to Carrie practice!

I had noticed that Fred would go downstairs whenever we practiced, but I didn't attach any significance to it. Then, today I asked him why he did that. He answered, "Well, I don't want to make a big deal out of it, but I can't stand the sounds that Carrie makes on that violin!"

That struck me as odd, because although I'm sure Carrie makes her share of squeaks and squawks, I haven't really been aware of them. Maybe that's because I have been concentrating on helping her get her thumb bent, or her nose and toes pointing the same direction. I guess it is my involvement in her practice that makes the difference.

Fred would go downstairs whenever we practiced.

January 21

Mrs. Wirth suggested I read *In the Suzuki Style,* so I did. I know now what's been missing in our practices — a sense of humor and an element of fun. We were making practices into a task to be done. We were taking it and ourselves too seriously.

No doubt about it, the practice time has to be a time of disciplined work, but a sense of anxiety over progress and the push for perfection can be deadly. We need to have some FUN along the way!

P.S.   Things are going better!

January 23

Suzuki violin people have a vocabulary all their own, I'm discovering. A large part of it is the repertoire itself — "Is your daughter working on the Boccherini yet?" "No, she is doing the 'Minuet in G.'"

"Did you hear the Olsen boy play the Seitz? He's marvelous!"

And then there's the thing called "Stevens Point."

"Are you going to Stevens Point this year?"

"Well, the kids want to go, and so do I, but we went last year, so I'm not sure."

Of course, there is also the vocabulary that has to do with violins in general — rosin, shifting, wrist vibrato.

I imagine I'll get with it as time goes on, but I do wonder, what's Stevens Point?

The Promises of Spring

February 2

Spring is coming . . . and so is Dr. Suzuki. I could hardly believe it when someone told me! I never thought that I would get a chance to see him, and now I will. He'll be here for the Suzuki Festival in April, which will be held in the auditorium on the University of Minnesota campus. I don't know if Carrie is excited, but I surely am.

Actually, I was stunned to realize that Carrie didn't know that Suzuki was the name of a flesh and blood person. When I told her Dr. Suzuki was coming, she said, "Who's he?" So I got out my copy of *Nurtured by Love* and showed her some pictures of him. I told her that she would get to play for him. That frightened her for a moment until I assured her that she would be in a large group, and that Dr. Suzuki loved children a lot.

Having that as a goal to look forward to has certainly improved our practices. The trick is to help her do her best without communicating my own anxiety to her.

P.S. We have decided to try to get "May Song" done by the time Dr. Suzuki comes.

February 6

News Flash! Scott is back! I sat down by his mother in group today. She smiled and said, "Well, here we are again."

"Oh, did Scott change his mind about playing?" I asked.

"We quit because Scott didn't seem very motivated," she said. "Practicing was always a struggle and I just got tired of it all. But the funny thing is, we both missed it when we weren't doing it any more. I mean, we weren't exactly setting the world on fire, but it was important to both of us."

"I know just what you mean," I said. "Sometimes I think I just can't do it, but I don't want to do without it."

"The worst part for me was sitting here imagining that everyone was a page right out of the book when I felt like we were just barely progressing. But we're going to hang in there this time."

"Listen, you don't need to feel intimidated by us, I can tell you that! We're in this together, and anytime you feel like you've just had it, give me a call. We can commiserate with each other!"

February 11

"The time has come," the walrus said, "To speak of many things, of ships and shoes and sealing wax, *and bribing my child to play strings.*" That's my version of the little verse from "Through the Looking Glass." Call it encouragement, offering incentives, giving rewards, bribery, I'm doing it! And it seems to make all the difference. I suppose I shouldn't be surprised. To expect a child to exercise discipline, to concentrate and to put up with a certain amount of pain for the pure joy of doing is ridiculous. Adults don't even do that, at least not very often.

I have thought about this a lot. Children can't look far into the future and choose their actions to lead to a remote end. They function on the visible, tangible, now result. For Carrie, part of that is just having her mother to herself. (Sometimes. Other times she hates me to be with her when she practices.) Praise for her real accomplishments gives her a boost, and she likes playing for her grandparents when they visit, but a new hair ribbon, a scratch-and-sniff sticker, or a cone at the Dairy Queen seem to motivate her more.

February 16

I bought the accompaniment tape, and it has really been a lot of fun for Carrie to play with it. She has had to work very hard on tempo, and there have been some tears, but she's been willing to do it because when she plays with the tape, it sounds "just like the record."

"The time has come," the Walrus said.

February 17

Carrie has been playing for our company lately. She does a good job (I think) and I am so proud of her. But I wonder what she sounds like to them. Depending on how willing they are to share her excitement and her sense of accomplishment, her performances could be either marvelous or disastrous.

Maybe I'm just over-sensitive about it. And no wonder. The "precocious performer" is the butt of cartoons, jokes, stories and half-hidden smiles. How do I know if our guests really enjoy it, or just put up with it, only to complain to each other after they've left?

I would never want Carrie's enjoyment of playing to be dampened by my doubts, either. If she senses reservation on my part, she will begin to doubt herself and that would be reflected in every aspect of her playing.

I wish I had an answer to this.

February 20

Stevens Point: *Noun, name of a town in Wisconsin;
location of a branch of the University of
Wisconsin; location of the oldest (but
not the only) Suzuki Institute in the
United States . . . Name is used to refer
to town or to the institute inter-
changeably. "I'm going to Stevens
Point" can mean, "I'm going to a town
in Wisconsin," or "I'm going to the
Suzuki Institute."*

As you can see, part of my confusion has been cleared
up. The Suzuki Institute at Stevens Point is held in
August of each year and revolves around music—
individual lessons, group lessons, theory, concerts, talent
shows and practice.

It sure sounds as though it would be fun. Of course,
part of the attraction is simply having some place to go
where I don't have to cook or do any of the other
thousand things that go into keeping a household
running smoothly.

I am going to check into it further when the flyers
come out for this year's program.

Practicing

February 22

Mrs. Wirth says the ideal lesson breakdown is 20 minutes on review, and 10 minutes on current material. Here's our actual lesson breakdown:

5 minutes — getting Carrie from where she is to where we practice.

5 minutes — getting out violin, tightening bow, rosining bow.

4 minutes — finding sponge.

2 minutes — asking "why" questions: Why do I have to do this? Why do you have to be here? Why can't I play just one song?

3 minutes — tonalization. (Don't let that fool you — it takes that long to do it just once.)

1 minute — scratching various spots.

5 minutes — review. (This should not be understood as 5 consecutive minutes.)

3 minutes — new material. (This should not be understood as 3 consecutive minutes.)

2 minutes — putting violin away.

Does this add up to 30 minutes of *practice*?

February 25

I hear Dr. Suzuki has asked his students to do a particular exercise as many as 5,000 times! Can you believe it! That is way beyond what we'll ever do, but I'm going to start a 25 Club, a 50 Club, a 75 Club, and a 100 Club. The idea will be to get Carrie to work on a problem spot more willingly. If she does something 25 times a week, she would qualify for the 25 Club. If she does something 50 times, she would qualify for the 50 Club, etc.

A MacDonald's gift certificate, some colored plastic paper clips, or a new notebook could be the membership award for the 25 Club or 50 Club, with maybe something more substantial for the 75 and 100 Clubs. After all, to do something 100 times a week would mean doing it 14 times a day plus two extra! That's a big order for a small girl! Perhaps the activity of her choice would be a good award — going to a show, the zoo, or a concert.

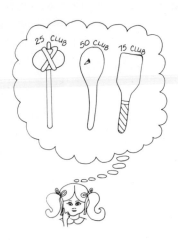

What club do you qualify for?

February 27

Sweatshirt message I saw at group lesson today: *Suzuki mothers don't yell.*

Oh, yeah? Just yesterday Mrs. Wirth told me about an incident she had with her daughter. The daughter was being sassy, so Mrs. Wirth "raised her voice" in reprimand. (Doesn't that sound more genteel than "Yelled?") Anyway, that didn't faze the daughter a bit. She just delivered the ultimate put-down: "You sure don't sound like a Suzuki mother!"

I'm afraid there are times when I don't either. But then, I'm just a novice. I haven't taken my final vows yet!

Anyhow, yelling is a way of life for me. Some people work off tension and frustration by jogging. I yell. Very therapeutic. And it's the only way I can get my kids to listen to me. Oh, yes. I know. They don't answer unless I yell because I'm always yelling. One of those vicious circles. But as yet no one has instituted a "Screamers Anonymous."

And the life of a closet screamer is terrible. Always putting on the front of a soft-spoken, genteel suburbanite when one has the soul of a fishwife is not easy. I know that there is a whole subculture of yellers and screamers out there too embarassed to admit their shortcoming. I sure wish they would. I get a bit lonesome. And when I'm lonesome, I yell louder. And it's always the same word: HELP!

March 3

We've been putting a lot more music into our lives lately — listening to good FM stations, tuning in the *Great Performances* series on Public Television, even going to a concert by the Suburban Symphony. And we are slowly building our collection of classical records.

Music sure can make a difference in my mood. No matter how I'm feeling when I start to listen, I always feel better after a while. It takes my mind off the problems of the day and satisfies a need like nothing else can.

I remember reading an article which stated that children who hear a certain piece of music over and over again when very young tend to turn to that music for comfort the way other children turn to blankets and thumbs. Now, if I could only learn to use music in place of oral gratification, I'd be 10 pounds lighter!

March 5

Carrie made the 25 Club — not as hard as she thought. Five times a day for five days did it! We gave her some new red hair ribbons, and she was very pleased. It sure worked a lot better as a motivator than the "Solve a Problem" sign!

March 6

About playing for guests: Everyone has a hobby he enjoys sharing with others—music is ours.

Yes, I realize that my friends may not feel the same way I do about Carrie's violin playing, but sharing is important in itself. Even when I am not interested in a friend's hobby *per se*, I still can enjoy his enthusiasm and involvement, and appreciate his effort, if not his expertise. I know my friends can do the same for me.

So Carrie will go right on playing for guests, with this concession: I'll try to limit the number of songs she plays to two or three. If I left it up to her, she'd play every song she knows!

March 10

Mrs. Wirth has encouraged the parents to bring their children to individual lessons a little early. That way, we can watch someone else's lesson and learn from it as well. So today we went early and arrived as Jon L. was having his lesson. Yuck. I think I will have Carrie watch the lesson *after* hers next week, instead of the one before. This kid — well, I just don't want to believe he's real. He is a kindergartener, supposedly a beginner, but he is playing one of the Bach minuets!

I asked his mother when he started and she said, "Oh, this summer during summer school."

"How did he get so far in such a short time?"

"He just taught himself. I haven't been pushing him at all."

I almost said, "I suppose he toilet-trained himself at 9 months too," but I restrained myself. Still, I knew there had to be something else operating that she hadn't yet mentioned. And by the end of our conversation I knew at least part of what it was.

This little boy has two sisters in the program. He has been watching them play since he was three. He has been hearing the tape for two years. No wonder he was so ready to play! It has to make a difference to have that kind of exposure when so young.

Even so, I can't help but think that he is unusual. Dr. Suzuki says that all children can learn to play violin. The difference is that some need only five repetitions, others fifty, others five-hundred. I believe that and it helps, but it sure would be nice if my kid were one of the "fivers."

March 13

Well, our club idea for motivation has worked fairly well, although the 75 and 100 Clubs are really out of Carrie's reach, if the time limit is one week or if the problem spot is long. But when we extend the time to two weeks on a particular problem spot, she reaches her goal and feels really proud of her playing!

But no single idea is the all-time cure for motivation. Soon I will need to come up with something else. I've noticed that Carrie really likes the little "bow creatures" that some kids have. They are cute little furry creatures with a spring inside. They can be clipped to bows, collars, sweaters, just about anything. I think the skunks are cute, but she really likes the raccoons. Maybe I'll get a raccoon and have it set aside for a day when things seem a bit down.

P.S.   I found some in a book and stationery store, and also in the *Miles Kimball Catalogue.*

March 17

We're on a high. We have been practicing a lot, and working on problem spots. We're trying to get everything polished for Dr. Suzuki's visit, even though Carrie will only be playing selected numbers. It's wonderful what the proper motivation will do!

We've had good group lessons and we'll have a district play-through before the festival.

P.S. It occurred to me as I wrote the above that to call part of a song a problem spot might contribute to its being a problem. But what can I call it?

I've got it! I remember what my piano teacher used to call such spots: Fractures. A fracture is a part of a song that is weak, or "broken." But playing it over and over again helps it to become the strongest part of the song.

I always have Carrie play a problem spot — oops! — a fracture five times in a row. Maybe she'd like a little equation: F × F = F (Five × Fracture = Fabulous).

March 21

Carrie didn't put her violin away before going to school today — so I just left it out. I wanted to see how long it would take her to get the picture and put it away. Well, I got the picture instead. She picked it up three times between the time she came home from school and bedtime, each time playing one or two songs. That added up to at least 15 minutes more practice time.

I'd like to leave it out, if I could find a place relatively safe, yet easy for Carrie to reach.

P.S. The violin is on third shelf of the bookcase. Matt has been told not to touch it without asking. I hope he doesn't decide it's a toy . . . .

March 25

Matt got Carrie's violin down today and proceeded to "play" while singing the repertoire songs. He's sure he's playing what he's singing! I hate to disillusion him. He shows great interest in violins and can tell when there is violin music on the radio, notices them in pictures, and bows with the tape using anything handy. He has learned a lot just by watching Carrie, listening and going to group lessons with me. He will really be ready to start next year when he goes to kindergarten.

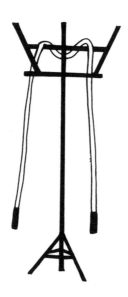

Dr. Suzuki's Here!

April 15

What a day! If I hadn't been to other Suzuki concerts where chaos gradually gives way to order, and order to beauty, I would have just gone home.

In the first place, it seemed as though there were thousands of children there. And adding the parents and siblings of the violinists, violists, cellists and bassists, the whole place was pandemonium. The auditorium floor was packed during the rehearsal, and both floor and balcony were jammed at concert time.

We got there early in the morning, found seats, and got Carrie's violin tuned. Then we waited for Dr. Suzuki to arrive. What a diminutive person he is! And how vital, considering his age. How vital, no matter what the age! He just sends out waves of energy in all directions.

The energy was understandable in any language, but his comments . . . well, that's another thing altogether. I must confess, it was the first time I ever heard someone from Japan speak English with a German accent! Luckily for me, I know some German and that knowledge helped me to understand Dr. Suzuki when a good percentage of the people around me couldn't.

Well, he started with the advanced groups and worked downward. He had a teaching point to relate to each song, and it was fascinating to see him work with the children on this point. I was surprised at how quickly time went and how soon Carrie was on stage with her group. Not that I could see her. She was somewhere by the piano, behind about 75 kids. But then, she was in front of another 50! Unbelievable! I wonder if she really experienced the presence of Dr. Suzuki? When I asked her what she thought of it, she said it was all right, and Dr. Suzuki was "O.K." Ah, well. She's only six.

When the groups were done, we decided to go eat. Basically a sound idea. We went to *Pizza Hut*. Not so sound. One should never eat salty food before a concert. By the time we got back to the auditorium and had found some seats, we were so thirsty we were miserable. Carrie kept wanting another drink. Nothing the matter with that, since our seats were on the aisle close to the door and a fountain. But three drinks add up to one bathroom trip. And the bathrooms were a light-year away. So there we sat, waiting for things to get organized; tired, hot, thirsty and in Fred's case, disgruntled.

But when the concert finally got started, the music was so wonderful that all the frustrations were forgotten. Well, almost all. We still had certain side-trips to deal with. But it was thrilling to hear all those children play! As each group was called, the children would line up in the hall and then go on stage. But there were so many violinists, that the older students had to leave the stage to make room for the younger. By the time we got to the "Twinkles," they were lined up in the aisles on the floor and in the balcony. We had stereophonic sound! One thousand five hundred violinists playing "Twinkle, Twinkle Little Star". Of course, I cried. And Fred was captivated also.

I spent the next few days trying to figure out what made Dr. Suzuki seem so special to me. And then it occurred to me that it was his great love. It just crossed over the language barrier and cut through the crowds. We were there to celebrate him, but he was there to celebrate us.

April 21

Thank heaven for parents' meetings. They really pick me up! After all, there are other Suzuki mothers who feel inadequate and whose children have decided they hate violin! Someone suggested that it may not be the violin Carrie was hating, but someone or something else. So the next time she got upset, I used the "feedback" technique.

"You really have strong feelings right now."

"This violin stuff is dumb."

"You don't sound like you're enjoying playing."

"Oh, I like to play. It was fun when Amanda was playing too."

"You liked playing with Amanda."

"Yes, but she quit. *Her mother let her quit!* She's not like you!"

"Sounds like you miss having Amanda in group lesson."

"Ya, I do. It's no fun any more. I'd rather go to Amanda's and play."

"You miss Amanda and want some time to play with her, right?"

"Uh huh."

"Would you like to play with Amanda on Tuesday? Then you wouldn't miss her so much at group."

"Oh, yes! I'd like that!"

"O.K. We'll call her mother and set it up as soon as we're done practicing. Let's see, we were on 'Allegro,' weren't we?"

Whew!!!!!

April 24

We're thinking about going to the institute at Stevens Point. I'm excited about it and so is Carrie. At least she is now. At first she was just confused, she had no idea what I was talking about. But when I told her she would be able to meet a lot of kids her own age who play the violin, she decided it might be fun.

Everyone I've talked to has had good things to say about their experience at Stevens Point. They've all mentioned how much the kids liked being with others who are doing the same thing they are. And how motivated they are being surrounded by music.

And I hear the food is *great*, especially the ice cream!

Actually, the only criticisms I've heard at all is that the dorm rooms are stifling and that the institute is very large. It is not unusual to have over 1,000 students there in any given week. But it is the closest to us, so that's where we'll go.

April 26

Boy, did I lose my temper today. Carrie was in a snit, and when I tried to remind her of what Mrs. Wirth had said to do in certain parts of the song, she would say, "No, she didn't. I was there. I heard everything she said, and she didn't ever say that!"

So, I patiently tried to explain why each point was important, but of course, logic didn't work. Patience didn't work either, and finally all I had left was anger. I mean, after all, I was giving my time, my concentration, my concern and caring, and all I was getting back was a lot of lip!

At that point, I just took her violin away, and said, "You can't play when you are acting like that. You let me know when you are ready to play and we'll try again."

She didn't say a thing about her violin the rest of the day, but the next day our practice went without incident.

The Ideal and the Real

May 3

Today I was leafing through what I had written at the beginning of this adventure, and I came across the part where I said that I didn't know the "other side of the picture." Well, let me assure you, I know the other side now. The side nobody talked about.

The other side is reality. The Ideal and the Real, back to back, showing one face and then the other. The Ideal raising hopes, giving confidence and new enthusiasm; the Real using up hope, confidence, enthusiasm, and faith, so that one must turn again to the Ideal to be replenished.

Whenever I steep myself in the Ideal, it gives me the feeling that I can do it. I can be a better mother-coach. I can be more patient, more loving. I can do everything just like it is in the books. And I will!

But of course, I can't do it just like it is in the books. In spite of all my good intentions, I can't live up to the Ideal, because I am an individual with my own needs and problems, and my child is an individual with her needs and problems. Put us together and there emerges yet another set of problems! We haven't a prayer of living up to the Big Expectation in the Sky. And when that fact burrows in to stay, it is very discouraging. It makes me wonder why I bother.

Why, indeed. You know the child that taught himself "Lightly Row" at age four? That's not my child. The child that gets up every morning to play the violin because he "just loves it?" Not my child. The one that always cooperates willingly? Not mine!

Mine is the child who can't play today because her fingers hurt. Mine is the child that can't stand to be touched if I try to correct her bow hold. Mine is the child that goes to a concert and refuses to play.

But "Suzuki" is for me and my child too, no matter how far from the Ideal we seem to be. Dr. Suzuki didn't create an exclusive movement, one just for the elite or the very talented. It is for everyone and is perhaps of even greater value to those of us who have to struggle with it. For in struggling, we keep moving closer to the best we can be.

I need to remember that the number of songs Carrie learns, or the speed at which she learns them, isn't the most important part of what we are trying to accomplish together. The process itself is the most important: the day-to-day discipline, the day-to-day attention to detail, the day-to-day awareness of beauty in the world.

And I have to remember that on some days, Carrie is just as wonderful as the *Wunderkinder*: She has gotten up early just to practice (one day), she has learned some songs very quickly, she has played a few really musical notes since we started!

May 7

The songs are getting more difficult and longer now. Sometimes I doubt our ability to take that next step. But if I remember that it is just a step — one step at a time, as small a step as is necessary — we'll be O.K.

And the first step I need to take is a review of all the things I have learned about being a good mother-coach:

1. Be consistent about practice time.
2. Praise, praise, praise.
3. Enjoy the time with Carrie.
4. Listen, listen, listen.
5. Sing fingering charts.
6. Sing bowings while bowing over arm or shoulder.
7. Divide into sections.
8. Preview most difficult spots.
9. Allow Carrie all the time she needs in order to be successful.
10. Be happy.

May 9

I think I have a clue as to why the Japanese do so well with the Suzuki method. It lies in the Eastern philosophy that does not divide being from doing, or product from process. We Western minds split everything, with the result that we want the product but hate the process. Especially if it is long-term or demands personal discipline and change. The Suzuki process, in Eastern terms, has less to do with music than personal development. It involves changing the person, helping him to be better, more self-controlled, patient, sensitive, able to concentrate, etc. One could pick Zen archery or Yoga asanas to reach the same goal.

In this context, learning to play the violin becomes a matter of desire, quite unrelated to ego. The length of time involved in the process does not even come into question. And the songs become the means through which developing beauty of character is revealed.

I suppose that sounds strange, and is quite removed from the daily process (perhaps even in Japan), but it makes sense to me. If only I were able to translate concept into attitude and then into action, not only would the Suzuki practice change, my whole life would change.

May 13

We've got some information about the Stevens Point Suzuki Institute, and Carrie is starting to get excited. We talked to Mrs. Wirth about which level she should be in, levels being determined by the student's most advanced polished piece. She'll be grouped with other kids partly by level of achievement, partly by age. I'm glad to hear that. It reflects the growing realization that Dr. Suzuki's method is sound for all students, regardless of the age at which they begin. After all, Dr. Suzuki believes that all children can learn to play, it just takes some longer than others. And if snobbism doesn't creep into the program, then accommodations will be made for those who progress more slowly or who have special needs.

Well, so much for that.

Carrie will have three lessons a day. A group lesson, a theory lesson and an individual lesson. Sounds like a lot of work, but also a lot of fun. There's a pool, so she can swim if she wants to, and TV in the lounge. I doubt she'll be doing much watching, between eating, sleeping, going to lessons, practicing, swimming and going to concerts. We'll probably be too busy even to find out where it is!

May 20

I found a quote I like on the next to the last page of *Zen and the Art of Motorcycle Maintenance*[1], by Robert Piersig. The scene is a road in California, down which a father and son are riding on a motorcycle. The son begins the conversation:

> "Can I have a motorcycle when I get old enough?"
>
> "If you take care of it."
>
> "What do you have to do?"
>
> "Lots of things. You've been watching me."
>
> "Will you show me all of them?"
>
> "Sure."
>
> "Is it hard?"
>
> "Not if you have the right attitudes. It's having the right attitudes that's hard."

[1]Robert Piersig, *Zen and the Art of Motorcycle Maintenance: An Inquiry into Values.* New York: Bantam, 1974.

June 3

Well, I let it all hang out, as they say. No more secrets, no more smooth facade. You know who I am, warts and all.

This last year has been hard in a lot of ways. I have had some crises of confidence that were very painful and Carrie's ups and downs have matched mine. There have been times when I felt like we were stuck in a hole and would never get out again.

It has not been easy to add Suzuki violin to our already busy lives. But surprisingly, it has not been just one more thing to do, like another swimming class, for example. It has affected all of us in a positive way.

You know how many times I have been ready to toss the whole thing. But I haven't, because Carrie does love it (in spite of frequent disclaimers) and I think it is important for all of us. So we keep chugging along, with the help of Mrs. Wirth, the tape, various books and the support of other mothers.

I saw a picture in a copy of the Suzuki Journal which showed a girl on a bicycle with her violin. The caption was "Dr. Suzuki would say, 'Don't hurry, but don't stop, either.'"

I guess that says it all.

Bibliography

Bigler, Carole L., and Valery Lloyd-Watts. *Studying Suzuki Piano: More Than Music*. Athens, Ohio: Ability Development Associates, Inc., 1979.
A comprehensive coverage of what the Suzuki approach embodies, particularly in the study of piano. The authors give their ideas about what it takes to be a Suzuki teacher, how to structure an effective lesson, what to cover in those first lessons, and how to do it. Using more than 400 musical examples, the teaching points and interpretations of the six volumes of Suzuki Piano School music are presented. Comparisons with traditional and original editions are offered. This 8½ by 11 inch book is a must for pianists of any level. Translated into Japanese and German. 265 pp.

Hermann, Evelyn. *Shinichi Suzuki: The Man and His Philosophy*. Athens, Ohio: Ability Development Associates, Inc., 1981.
A biography of Suzuki recounting his family background and the cultural setting in which he grew up. Seven sons and five daughters of the Suzuki family were virtually raised in a violin factory. Famous people greatly influenced his life. A fascinating chain of events led ultimately to his development of the philosophy we know as Talent Education. Many photographs and documents from the family album are reproduced. The second half of the book is a rare source of his addresses and papers, both philosophical and pedagogical. This is a book to treasure for all who admire Suzuki. 5½ by 9 inches, 253 pp.

Koppelman, Doris. *Introducing Suzuki Piano*. San Diego, California: Dichter Press, 1978.
A concise and introductory description of Suzuki's Talent Education method and how it applies to the teaching of piano. 5½ by 8½ inches, 112 pp.

Landers, Ray. *The Talent Education School of Shinichi Suzuki—An Analysis: The Application of Its Philosophy and Methods to All Areas of Instruction*. Third Edition. Smithtown, New York: Exposition Press, 1984.
Probably the most comprehensive coverage and analysis of Suzuki's Talent Education method available under one cover. An effort is made to convey to the reader insights into the Suzuki method which will help him appreciate the universality and soundness of its ideals. A broad range of criticisms and misinterpretations of the system are traced and discussed. Much practical information is included about the establishment of programs and how to work with the piano pedagogy. Modern learning theories are defined and compared to Suzuki's ideas. An excellent resource and reference book. 6 by 9 inches, 189 pp.

Mills, Elizabeth, and Suzuki Parents. *In the Suzuki Style: A Manual for Raising Musical Consciousness in Children.* Berkeley, California: Diablo Press, 1974.
A source book of ways for parents to bring musical activities and experiences to their children. Ideas from parents are practical and workable. Teachers offer tips on a variety of topics—tuning, recordings, holiday songs, travel, summer activities. Delightfully illustrated. 5½ by 8½ inches, 120 pp.

———, Shinichi Suzuki, and others. *The Suzuki Concept: An Introduction to a Successful Method for Early Music Education.* Berkeley, California: Diablo Press, 1973.
An overview of Suzuki's philosophy and principles. Although it is one of the earliest book-length publications about Talent Education, it continues to earn its recommendation as an introductory text for anyone interested in the Suzuki movement. A convincing and strongly reassuring discussion of the rote approach and delayed note-reading is particularly relevant for traditionally trained musicians. 5½ by 8½ inches, 216 pp.

Slone, Kay Collier. *They're Rarely Too Young and Never Too Old "to Twinkle": Teaching Insights into the World of Beginning Suzuki Violin.* Lexington, Kentucky: Life Force Press, Inc., 1982.
An overview as well as specific information of what takes place while young violin students prepare to perform their first piece, "Twinkle, Twinkle, Little Star." This stage, known as Pre-Twinkle, consists of many small learning steps that must be expertly dealt with by the teacher and parent, and it generally involves far more than most people envision. This book describes the step-by-step approach of this particular author based on her personal experience with the Suzuki method, and it offers many ideas for teachers to consider. 5½ by 8½ inches, 218 pp.

Starr, William and Constance. *To Learn with Love: A Companion for Suzuki Parents.* Knoxville, Tennessee: Kingston Ellis Press, 1983.
As performers, teachers and parents, the Starrs share their experiences and insights gained during many years of involvement with the Suzuki movement. Just as the Suzuki method deals with the whole child, this book covers all of the subjects that the Starrs feel are important in a family's growth. It includes chapters on practice, concentration, motivation of both the young child and the high school student, sibling rivalry, nutrition, and more. Helpful information from a pianist and violinist on special topics involving music instruction is given. A meaningful text for all who interact with children of any age. 5½ by 8½ inches, 242 pp.

Starr, William. *The Suzuki Violinist: A Guide for Teachers and Parents.* Knoxville, Tennessee: Kingston Ellis Press, 1976.
A book written, according to the author, for those least informed about the Suzuki philosophy and methodology. Sections are devoted to all the significant elements of the approach, particularly those dealing with the

violin and how it is taught. Although the Suzuki pedagogy continues to evolve, this text is still timely in its detailed descriptions of the application of the method. It is well illustrated and especially recommended for teachers. 8½ by 11 inches, 142 pp.

Suzuki, Shinichi. *Ability Development from Age Zero.* Translation by Mary Louise Nagata. Athens, Ohio: Ability Development Associates, Inc., 1981.
Written not long after *Nurtured By Love*, this book is based on Suzuki's belief that "the fate of a child is in the hands of his parents." It embodies all of the philosophical principles of Talent Education and emphasizes the adult's responsibility to improve everything under his control and create an environment worthy of the noble spirit with which every child is born. It includes many anecdotes and much inspirational food for thought. Written particularly for parents who seek suggestions about interacting with their children. 5½ by 8½ inches, 96 pp.

————, *Nurtured By Love.* Translated by Waltraud Suzuki. Smithtown, New York: Exposition Press, 1969.
This book is the cornerstone of any Suzuki-oriented library. Suzuki, a world-renowned violinist and educator, introduces the philosophy and principles of his teaching methods for developing the natural abilities of every child. Through examples from his own life and teaching, he establishes his case for early childhood education. Convincing evidence is presented to substantiate that every child is born with high potential that will be realized only if the opportunity is present in his environment. The text is somewhat autobiographical and makes fascinating reading. It's a *must.* 5½ by 8½ inches, 121 pp.

————, *Where Love is Deep.* Translated by Kyoko Selden. St. Louis, Missouri: Talent Education Journal, 1982.
A collection of articles arranged into three groups. The first section deals with the author's fundamental ideals of Talent Education, and the second with instructions for application, particularly in the area of string playing. The third section features open dialogues and discussion of various aspects of the Suzuki approach. The diversity of the writings makes this a fascinating book for both layman and Suzuki specialists. 6 by 8 inches, 149 pp.

Wilson, Charlene. *Teaching Suzuki Cello: A Manual for Teachers and Parents.* Berkeley, California: Diablo Press, 1980.
The author draws on her own teaching expertise as well as that of her colleagues in presenting a step-by-step manual to aid in teaching violoncello the Suzuki way. Beautifully illustrated, it is a helpful guide for teachers and parents with children involved in studying cello. 5½ by 8½ inches, 124 pp.

The books listed above, and other Suzuki-related materials, are available from Ability Development®, P.O. Box 4260, Athens, OH 45701-4260, U.S.A.